D1594182

LET'S NOT CALL IT CONSEQUENCE

MAY 0 8 2009

Columbia College Library
600 South Michigan
Chicago, IL 60605

LET'S NOT CALL IT CONSEQUENCE

RICHARD DEMING

Published in the United Kingdom in 2007 by Shearsman Books Ltd
58 Velwell Road
Exeter EX4 4LD
www.shearsman.com

ISBN   978-1-905700-66-0

Copyright © Richard Deming, 2008.

The right of Richard Deming to be identified as the author of this work has
been asserted by his in accordance with the Copyrights, Designs and Patents
Act of 1988. All rights reserved. No part of this publication may be reproduced,
stored in a retrieval system, transmitted in any form or by any means, electronic,
mechanical, photocopying, recording or otherwise, without the prior permission
of the publisher.

DESIGN Megan Mangum, Words That Work
AUTHOR PHOTO Jean-Jacques Poucel

Grateful acknowledgment is made to the editors of the magazines where some of these poems first appeared: *A. Bacus, Colorado Review, Damn the Caesars, Elevator, Free Verse, Kiosk, The Little Critic, Mandorla, Mirage (Period)ical #4, Shearsman, Queen Street Quarterly,* and *Word/for Word.* "Annus Miriabilus" appeared as part of *Led Astray by Language,* a chapbook assembled by Simon Cutts and Erica Van Horn and published by Coracle.

The author wishes to thank David Lynch for his generous permission to use the cover photograph.

TABLE OF CONTENTS

I.

II.

III.

I.

A FRAGMENT OF ANYTHING YOU LIKE

1.

This voice
        scattered and lifelike.

 She stood
           in the doorway, watching.
"What," she asks, "is the first thing you remember?"

Rough sided shoulder bones
       click and pop out of place.

Transformation slows into
       the Atlantic Ocean
       and there's no proving it.

The stones along the river are empty mouths.
                         Asthmatic.

2.

The glance upwards.

See, sky never abandons.

Begs each day's mournful
constancies.

The slats of a tanning bed:

               light from a meridian fluency.
         But you know what   he means
         if the stranger doesn't mention atrocity.

Okay, now say what you came here for:

To stitch a crescent understanding.
                    The unleavened impressions,
oily smear of doubt against a white hot bulb and thus

to ache, so to speak,
is human.

It is, for instance, (an instant)
Autumn. Leaves spill
          and cover
     condom wrappers and cast-off shoes.
Kindergarteners drag their feet and leaves make it
sound like rain. Or, sound like *sound*. Or, sound.
What to use to cover things up.

Helicopters circle the neigh-
          borhood all night. Search
lights move through
          the hallways of my apartment. The blades' whir
washes out the music from
          the CD player—Bach's *Matthäus-Passion.*

Arias to drown out sirens,
          drown out police boats dragging the river,
               drown out raccoons rummaging through bins
               filled with vodka bottles and rotten artichoke hearts.

                         Daily
sufferings arrange the day with a sudden composition.
          Stones thrown from the 5th Ave. bridge sink into the
Scioto, (or *x*)
          (let *x* stand for the Scioto River running through
Columbus, OH)

into the sludge at the bottom. No one swims
          in *x*, at least
not in Columbus.

Let y now stand for the Erie canal, as in "I used to live near y
where no one swims because once a kid jumped from a trestle
and dove right through the bloated corpse of a cow that had
been trapped when the locks were refilled in the spring."
For every $y = x$, and every x
must have its day.

      Still suffering
accrues, cannot be obscured, becomes a wideness
      in which a cathedral springs up. What serves as votive
prayer in such a place, where love is a kind of reckoning, where
the Virgin's hand curves into a question mark?
      Borne along (*a wanting*) by a dread velocity—
            naveward (*a hunger*), then down to the river
            once more
down to the basket caught in the rushes, as the pharoah's
daughter plucks x from the water,
      lifts y into her arms so that all substitutions will
          again
               begin
         again,
and looking never
is explanation and this is
      what aphasia would be (like),
each alphabet spirited away,
          what would you stop it if you could
      and now where is there
to look away from,

where is *not now*? Only *here* as a limb
                              slips

            from the river bed, gauzy with moss, its final
Dickinsonian angle catches the bank and the insistent
logic of green will,
                    for singularity's sake,
                                    suffice.

OH

The beautiful mouth
      a flame
            again,
shape of such ache
            and plenty.

Disastrous intent,

reckon your ascent
in scares and feeble
unforgivings. What's the use of ladders

anyways? Climbing's too far.

The hand doesn't care.
The ear doesn't know.
The leg's done in.

This is the part where you laugh.
Piece it
together and I
promise the tongue will
take it apart.

SOME KINDS OF LOVE ARE MISTAKEN
FOR VISION

Her face, opened, like a mirror.
In the forgetfulness of touch
other places appear.

Three scurry home in a wind storm towards a toothless door.

Edges of even (if)
no one lives that way anymore, present
and accounted for. Or at least you think.

The kettle water begins to boil over,
its frothy whitening of the stove's top sends
one back to those moments of
insistence
and cost. *I meant almost
every word.*

That is to say, how'd
we come
to this—tumbled back to get ahead, to where the bookmark
gives the self one more bastion
of timeliness. What we do for love. Or lack thereof.

A fattened finch circles the belltower, its beak unhinged.

Matter/No matter. Rather,
what keeps
us
here?
Such rangeless environs. All eyes offered.
If the water were any deeper, I'd still drown
myself all
over again.

"IN THIS PORTION LOVE HAS NO SOLID GRIP"

I've seen your hand
        slide saintly across
a painted cheek.

If setting out were some cadenza,
it'd be finished soon enough,
        the fraught

absence of you,
let me count the ways.

This mind, all that's mine,
its terrifying vertigo,
        the light sings the canvas
in a yellow, blue arc.

And who would rather will
        nothingness than not
        will? A man
                    drives a bus
             into a plate glass window.
The nosebleeds and broken finger nails, a severed ear lies
parenthetic
in the raw grass, near the park.

        The house is quiet
        to be about
late afternoon, the coffee gone cold
        and forgetful,
        and the floorboards are rough and in bare feet
        the splinters
        go deep, to the bone. This measure of how far

        from me to there, matters enough.
        Picture:
timid, timorous, a third word that we do not recognize.
A vocabulary to figure distance.

How you say…I'm not here now,
leave a message.
I want an answer more generous than this,
since meaning is no machine, but a luck

        good as the promise
                of a brief, almost beautiful world.

IN CASE OF EMERGENCY

        Stay with me lexicon, until morning

when dawn's the boundary music
            by which to sound
action. Or thing.
If there's a difference,
let's kiss.

.

ON FIRE
—*After Heraclitus, for Tom Meyer*

Darkened tooth of my each decade,
          which want would
guide us to home?

A river forgets its occasions.
Fire is remembrance: ash, bone, smoke against skin.

Then, what and is
          any ever
ever enough? Listening all night, perhaps, or
the taste of bread, so
               sweet and without guile it stuns
               the mouth all the way
                              to the North Sea.

WHEREBY

A friend hands back a white page saying, *I circled*
where you've said almost enough.

Fourfold excesses, the music of indecision.
Intimations of disentanglement : the way out.

Thorns inscribe the legs and forearm.
Teach me, won't you, to be useful.

The tongue's a muscle for reckoning.
                        And sleep does not come.

           I have been well accustomed these past days
               to detach my mind from my senses.

Open the door and *see.*
How near is
knowledge,

this is a room I know this is a room
           the mind is its own place
                    and the stove cool to the touch

and
the common ground of "what
           was it you
said?" opens and swallows
parked cars and playgrounds. Alright,
have half and the rest set adrift in a wicker basket.

In flesh's tender strain, intention is no paraphrasable weight,
nor nearly fluent.

Night's out of joint
and with the incessant
        din of insomnia, reason's a dog to kennel.

How to be disinterred from nothing.

If only
       this thinking thing thought thoughts only

what is the cost of shame
if I said what I wanted what
          would you do? The rue-
            ful hour,
such as it is, blind
to confession, comes too late.

 Because what can come between
      us is, also,
          philosophy.

An unearthing.
Eyelids flutter and close.

Wake to this, the reliquary, the enormous breath
     within which

the square of the hypo-
         tenuse entombs the house, in terms

anyone can
understand

its delicate, its single
aperture and no
words no words

until the walls revise the insistent elsewhere.

Mouths rush in all
      together.

What I wanted was a say:

Intention, tucked in, turns
      opaque.

As if at last, we could trust loveliness again.

But the slaughterhouse of noon parcels out
thankless intensities and a boy, smoke

eyes, burnt
ember skin stumbles out of an alleyway
cries, "I would tear the mother
in half. I would
            rip the mother fuck-
            er in two."

      The bitter taste of broken glass
      and the city's swollen belly.

      Otherwise, or
         so.

The body then sizes things up: arms outstretched,
Each breath haptic, seeing
         what's ahead
      by the tongue's elegant, insistent
                interrogations and the
cool hush

        of breath.

Could be: *"who knows?"*

Make it quieter, a lure, perhaps, of intimacy.
Let me I want to tell you…

The dream that someone writes the philosopher's
        name in yellow chalk,
                and the rain comes and no one cares.

But in sunlight is the emergent, the vatic
                blessings of found things,
that bark or sway, that History dresses in the fleshliness
        of entropy, and sodden leaves.

But now
in this moment, a bedtime
        story, would you
                trust to close your eyes:

bare interior, a tableau of shadows lengthening, then receding.
        A slow tumble towards dawn,

and the space
                around
the doorframe grows cold, and unconscionable.

In the dream you have of the dead, he says to himself, they come back and you've five minutes to spend with them, to ask of your life together, to ask why the heart is sometimes but not always a bird that feeds on bitter roots. It is night now, he says, and it should be better at this hour because the alleyways narrow and music carries beyond the rooftops but in the same dream the dead sit at picnic tables and eat cold sandwiches and drink wine intended for others.

It is an effort simply to arrive and ask open questions, isn't it, for anyone, let alone they who have come from deserted places, where memory is an empty ledger, and if we do not hear it is not for a want of listening. So far from silence, where will you place your hands? What one wants is sliced from the throat and placed in a small wooden box alongside a frayed ribbon, playing cards, nails, a shard of blue glass. An awful sea, distant every time, and the name that finds it, elsewhere.

II.

YOU SAID IT
— For Peter Gizzi

Tomorrow, it'll come
as it always does, forlorn
                    or done, you, that is, speaking.
        What I mean is,
what if we come back again
to this spot, finished with forgetting?
        But to forget is not the worst thing.

Right here and now I'd unflesh myself

as if syntax were the only hope. The brute
            given of loneliness, and the next right thing.
What would you give for certainty? The left eye is blue,
the right eye is gray, the nail catches
the skin of the forefinger, and the hill
                    is almost invisible in this
sordid light. *Okay?* Let me

                            have exactly one
                            failure and one
            success.

                    It's difficult, some-
                            times to know
                                how one
                        means.

The moon ministers the color orange.
The moon misuses us.

But the value of landscape is home.

Annihilation isn't all
it's cracked up to be, but

21

still it's something and so
                     gets jotted down in the notebook.

And the angry men in furious machines steal
bric-a-brac and the thought
                  that rings true.

     And then a race of onanists and blasphemers sprang
     from the local rivers, and we offered a Pythagorean
     theorem as a charm against the old ways.

Theoria as shroud, as compass to
solitude and breadcrumbs, as refuge
       from a terrible devouring.

       Did he just
              say Aristotle's skeleton is and is
                not a secret,
                      neither leers nor laments?

This broken music, a tin
              witness, good as any dream we'd invent.

ENMESH
—After Maya Deren, for Gerrit Lansing

Afternoon light seeps into doorjambs
                         and keyholes and reflects against
a knife's blade thrust halfway into a loaf
                         of warm bread.

Yesterday I dreamt another body
             and if I can wake, it means I'll have gone

             to sleep. The body, day traveler,
is not the only thing, the whole
story, but is where we
set out from, as we must.
             The mooring that entitles
             some certain return. The bluejay's shriek

startles the dark haired woman.
She turns from the open window.

Stepping backward, the occasion shatters
                                   into bits of stray film.
             Shutter speeds. Eyes open.
Everything I will ever love flickers
and catches. Unspools. Scratches the lens.

             Encase me in the daily. This too solid air
                   fashions a bright mirror.

POEM BEGINNING WITH A LINE
FROM *SWAMP THING*

empty spaces make empty gestures
          and to ask "and
how was your day" is to ligature and marrow

          look
          up, this
vegetative weight scars
          a pink arousal

the boy's back is rhomboid and dangerous
the wasp's stinger throbs as it crawls across an open palm

these only come by not arriving

          surprised by glass
the last hope left
          is an unlearning
a blotted and unreadable prose

this scatter frames a forgetfulness
               and a calling out
               that, in fact, calls
out

and in the degree
          zero of where the whole
               thing
stands, who's to say this is
or is not, Arizona say
or Alabama

a raven-complaint carries one point five miles,
               conjures from the slithery marsh

an arcane torso, its ragged hour come round
        shambling toward Baton Rouge

anecdotes of the last war
        counter-rhythmic punch lines
that rupture a good night sleep

some hero, massive and slow, appears too late
                                   and then

what comes next in this semblance of first to last

an arthritic hand leaves
small red marks about the nose, the eyebrows, the pallid fore-
head
        as the overture swells and down
                the street, any street, this steet even,
                        the blood from the crime scene
in front of the Rialto Theater blesses itself
        all the way to last week

taken by force,
                lament counts as insomnia

if there were any guttural plea
        the glint of a forgotten railroad tie
                carries it off

a haze of black flies thickens beneath magnesium streetlights.

J.'S NIPPLE RING

Wave, particle,

silver hoop held fast and hurtling.

Could I look without owning,

—*Pathways*
      teeth
a secretive tear—

I'd offer the price of this
      hidden architecture

aureole

its erect elaboration
what comes between.

Fleshy tuck and cleft, ontology, fingernails.

Held here,
the stammering of the cheek,
      eyelids, dissolution

what thing suggests, persuades

          hums its secret,
across the sternum—such inscription
                    —*who'd ever tell?*—
          pierces nerve endings
with a pain that claims its sources.

And if grace, as it can, comes inaudibly,

          let the nipple's dark   mouth be
                    perhaps
               its own unrelenting
                    response.

REMAINS TO BE SEEN

I wish I were the moon he said, with nothing
certain except what remains is the smoke
from far-off villages, and the question that lingers
of what did one come to expect of these
lives anymore? Tongue wanders, wonders, listless
              amidst cavities and contusions.
We never moved our eyes
from each other.

How much night needs a last cruel tune?
The blood in the porcelain sink,
                lit from above by a single bulb.
          The silver fixtures.

Tired and trebled, the sound afflicts more than sleep.
Wake the substitute, the odd order
of fledging witnesses to that wholly other
life found sidelong amongst reflections
                in a café window.
Add this promise to the luck of starting out.

Soot-covered song and factories all undone,
then the dream of red noses and floppy shoes
seems less than unreal.

He bared his throat to her, the glassy
flesh, its sudden and terrible
                distractions, rendering the present
                blind. Brick tears the fleshly cheek.
Then the dark underneath pushes fingernails into the heath.

What does it mean to forget the plot of every French film?
To resemble is to reassemble.

I own nothing but my own dead.

THE SOUND OF THINGS AND THEIR MOTION

All night, the blank page.
All night, the unopened book beat its black wings
against the glass, and I woke, forgetful.

Just like in the movies, the girl is there then gone,
each frame suspended midair.
This moment, wherever it finds us, is neither

mine nor yours.
A place with no
single word rises around

us with the bare
suddenness of a house,
wherein one finds

an unstained coffee mug, a cigarette burned to ash.
An iris rots in a vase above the fireplace.
Which *I* mattered, which earned its belonging?

The nerves, their gracless hum, now quieted.
At times the window and everything in it is blue.
The wish to damage and deny is its own season.

Unless an omen overwhelms the willow,
the pond is dried up and gone and every

proposition forgets the one before it. The camphor field

between grapes and echoes, blazes until its darkening.
Nothing candles the heart so
            much as loss.

Names tell me names to trace
the ways back

towards the saying of some
delicate,
some infinitely stuttering thing.

BUFFALO NIGHTS

starlit and ex-
cerpted it's colder
outside than
it looks

when the mirror gets heavy
and the chocolate
          stale, rust answers
          all that glare and some
          times sleep is a way of saying no

BY THE TIME YOU READ THIS...

And when at last the stars
     did not tremble
and the page would not take a desperate ink

the night, this rounded night, night of riot and thistle
     framed a place of re-entry, its humility
     a kind of fragrant desire. Such sleep as this.

     Be relentless, said the cold pear atop the formica table,
a wasp piercing its core, the mouth
a blackened rose, a bloom too much to bear.

DISTANCE

Just now it is not enough,
the bare
and brutal engine of the mind.
Marginalia,
the visible motion of bodies not there.

Betimes
the stenographer enters

the hallway (over and
done with answering)

and the eyelids glue themselves shut
against irresistible dictation.

There's a tune
        beyond geometry
                in which each
      line attach-
      es it-
self—scalene, isosceles—
to the ethics of standing apace.

The finger circles the brow, stops.

I've been listening the whole time.

Because of the snow
      the letter arrives too late.
            "The body doesn't want to know me anymore."

The sentence ends with a comma, and a blue sequined
      lampshade upturned.

Was it how you wondered it would be? Eyesight ascends
      towards what it knows.

What we cannot speak of
      must cover entire villages with ice.

Or was it that you forgot how
      you wanted it said?

Yellowed fingers stretch
      but the shutters remain open.

Inside your mouth
      take the tongue of forgetting—

its familiar alphabet with intimacy grows
      rough and scornful.

Chance narrows into
a crystal champagne glass
and each reflected face
is a blind turn.

Not even a song to offer a way back.

The tracks in the snow
        lead to a wall and a name spelled
           out with charcoal.

What was the word? The world?
        A wound that rhymes with promise.

I.

This sugared night,
the rain's a panic of you. I
can't even tell if my eyes
are closed.
                    What wins
with a kiss?
                              Everything to be
counted, to be lost.
            Bloodied or bartered
                the odd joints left out in the almost light,
bones unknit themselves, in an unwitting dark time.
Flower petals brittle and destitute.

There is a breath—then the blank

page of the turned face,
reckons any kind of ascent.
And this fair house is all that's left.

II.

To what noise
      will you give yourself?
Learning to love by subtraction, the skin
      tastes of milk-stench and silk.

This blindness begs a fitful prayer.
Destiny, vacant and portable, sleeps no hornet night.
The white planet on the table asks
                a lie, and I'll tell it.

I'm your nothing-man,
the foul rag thrown nowhere's safe.

III.

Amidst the prayer that would save the remaining
bruise of the present moment,
the molar bursts into flame
        and one of us, unnamed, unasked,
wills the airliner back into the sky
with the force of her mind,
        the gin and tonics all unspilled.

Remembering that poem
you wrote, your mouth
        familiar in the ways it untold the future.
Blood would be your erasure.

Repetition is eradication,
        said the dark bird, and I believed him. And this story
is a silence to be paid for, which

if it were true, would leave
the room as it is—
empty, standing.

IV.

What would you burn into your flesh?
Say *tongue*, say *begot*, say *cock*
Say *what remains*
Say *the old man* and say *the sea*
Say *the eidolons, the ideas, the patent leather shoes*
Say *night never comes,* say *my trousers are old*
Say *dark vein angling along the aureole*
Say *the gay science* and *the new science*
Say it loud say it soft
Say a dark insistent calligraph
Say none will hear, no one is near
Say who would bear the wound, articulate
   Say it'll hurt more than you

v.

Crucified in flesh and bone,
a vulgate of sparrows stuns the winter sky—
                                        its old

voice hidden
        beneath beating wings.

What cost this happenstance I,
        locus of the dead sun's mechanism
and an unreflecting word. Night from light,
true love from true
love, forgotten not made.

VI.

In a bleak midsentence,
sleeplessness is a height of medium blue.

Such sudden cold—
what is called
          thinking withdraws and there is no shock
the fingers, tip to tip, avoids.

What am I to you? What grammar
          of gates and dead letters beggars
                    the possibly visible. A voice named or not.

If it's darker past dawn, you measure the minutes
by drone and yaw.
If I lit my hand on fire, how
long would it burn you leave it all
to chance and it's been
so long, so
long that the leather bound book
begins to crack, and pictures,
yellowed and torn, make their way to the middle distance.

VII.

　　　From the magazine stands,
pop veneer crawls from glossy pages, jostled to the ground.

Blessed freight, glassine imago, teach me
what I'd almost been.
In the rising heat and play of light, I'll forget to be bored.

I'd wear a skull and bones, better late
than never, just to be part
of the plot. Hit and miss, you take your place
against the window, greased
over with handprints and
　　　stolen forgot-me-nots, and it's better
　　　this way is the order of the day.

Carry this whiteboned hope
and the road ahead remains a monster.

Burn the page where you are.

ANNUS MIRABILIS

One day when there is no breath, thus no longer song
no incantatory, forgiving algebra for the open window
          and the wind,
               and the wasps stirring along the sill
               in late March.

               Not cinder, not smoke, and what all
               else that will

        not be there. No more.
Is it enough, then, to glimpse another's
reflection in a picture window backed by night,
lit by Chilean wine and soft voices?
        The melon's syrup slicks someone's
cheek; a napkin thick with the scent
               of currants and folded in thirds
        falls to the floor.

Outside, the lawn furniture levitates above
        the sleepy eyes of mute animals led astray.
No other world but this. This.

III.

Knock, knock.

Who's there?

It is,
and so it is
not not a thing
of lonely and desiring bloom
        but violent
in its insistence—
as love will, as absence ought—

        the bruise to
follow all else.

Hello, thus.

THE NOW IS DAY

Before the cigarette's ashen end gives
         itself to freefall, you finger
a shadow puppet : a Germanic baroness
         at the end of the
Empire,

                  who doubts that whatever is
         possible is also crucial. Without

surprise or shock you could stumble
         your way outside of even

                           this sentence by which—in its
         naming—I am/you are
         bound—positioned like uncaptioned courtesans in
         a Madame Tussaud waxen tableau.

And yet, here we are, vaguely,
         if enough, so
                  what
                  can

you do? It would be easy
         to caterwaul just to feel

the throat's architecture, as blood vessels
                           knot then splay
         along the artery's

                  inky channels. The body's narrative
         unsays itself in the cellular

collapse of each night and Penelope
        unravels once more the tapestry

of arrival, of what's to come.
        But suppose each recitation

is the story's weaving and undoing
        so all that's left is

                the back and forth of fingers
        over the loom to invent

these dispersions. Such stammering hesitations of
        the definite—staccato,
    staccato. /   Each

        comma ticks like sleet against
        a windowpane. In the cold dawn

of allusion whole cities lurch forth
        and passion is driven into

the desert to live coiled around
        stones, biting its own tail.

THIS RIFT

fever lingers

and the city's collision
   shatters like fingertips

  what counts as perverse if
    the body be mistaken for the heart?

  that makes even
being burned
      alive seem viable and such is
my love that I would
even let you see my face as begins the desire
       to set your hair on fire
—just say it yes just once more—

my nipple, perhaps, is a wound
   or
a window, opened at your breath—
suppose a little man climbs inside there above
the ribs and falls asleep   then I am
a house, a habit, for this

sleeper, how else explain, this resistance

this gulf is the opposite of death
and a bruise, the measure of what is near

CORRESPONDENCES

In itself and for
itself, glass, cut
by hand and smoothed

      as fine turned and finite
      as need be.

A postcard placed along the window.

        Her dark sky
        of hair discovers

this stratum of
     being's
        here.

        Such *outside-it-all.*

               Let me point to it.

Cold,
the black pools of turning-towards, and again
      and again, thus
the terse thought unthinks it all.

         I'd anchor this to fact,
had today not lost its temper.

His head, lowered. This house, then —
      sudden, elliptic.

The glass, now cool against skin,
opens a small scratch beside the mouth.

Where stairs led astray
       thickets wracked the eye, and
pursuit sounds five leagues back.

             Occurrence is thorough: one
              iris, black and red
                  enough.

Let's talk to forget
       the ones we invent—each
             word—
and drape them anew with a stark sheet.

POLITICAL POEM

Awake, perforce

the machine we've built dreams
hyphenate suggestions, each gear thrumming
a consistent word. In the hour before
        dawn, a meadow beyond
the city is a ceasura
            edged by empty refrigerators and flaming trashcans.

At the diner counter in morning light,
a woman wishes each wound to scar, just to be
for once free from cruelty,
                moment by moment.
        To know
a little would be worth
        the cost of this
                    world.

If the lyric be dark,
I would bear any Soviet winter,
I would endure all night a desolate envy
            to arrive dead on the doorstep of those who offer
                    witness, they who do not want
the transmissible. Amid the troughs and heights,
                each thought
            a word, every kiss
an intimate syllable of want and home.

For you, the archive of lost ferocity burns
            one page at
            a time until
forgetfulness is an ashen cylinder

filled with broken teeth and failures no one claims, and even
the hungry men who prey on blue eyes and broken doorknobs
shutter the windows against what comes next.

This is a story not to tell and in time
the noise lures one to the river's shadowy shore
where flesh itself begins to hear as if underwater,
enough, but distantly.

Say
it is winter, and through the snow
a dark figure—a man—crosses
a bridge between you and there. Say
he stumbles back,
his pink tongue uncurls like a comma as he calls your name,
                              any name as he falls, that is if
he does, over the side, his scarf spread
above him like an upper lip, narrowing
against   the winter   sky.

How would you begin to describe
it with words hollowed out by sound?

And how does this occur to you later,
                    recur as syllables

and each vowel offers the place where you'd want
to invent a new opening
but there is no new place that lies
        fallow, unburdened
                    by appearance.

Instead you repeat to yourself: *The paddock door
is unlatched* or
        the burner
of the gas stove
        is wide open
and anxiety sets the world in motion:
                        an incantation for the universe
stretched taut like the brim of a bowler hat

into which Houdini pours
a pitcher of bourbon.

But memory is pixallated,
flickers horizontally and
                    (did you try
the vertical

                    hold?) the screen grows hazy
like the cigarette smoke darkening Rod Serling's
Botany 500 suit on a plastic black and white TV set.

Indirection as a means of accounting—the scarf
            was red, his boots
                            untied,
but yes you see still he did fall—and his fingers
splayed apart—as if the right details could quarry
            the moment before our eyes
but the truth
            is you can't really say
what belongs, can you?

So invent a plot by which he is brought
        to the edge of the bridge, which gives the authority
                                    for the figure to slip.

                Wait, did you make the whole thing up?
                    (It'd be so much easier if it made sense.)

Telling gathers, whatever its worth, the ordinary
and how we are fashioned—bewildered

by a language in which nothing appears or
            disappears, but draws

closer in—as the hushed crowd
        circles Houdini and his empty sleeves.

Think of a mirror would you as a shoring up of trust
as a place to start, a place to agree

sequins
spin and wobble across the bedroom floor

yessing this moment into the next—
(sequence)

What happened next? The reflection does not hold.
The facts interrogate the space of a moment

while you
woke and fell over woke and fell over
           the terror of partial knowledge

only to begin
      to begin again.

Now a quarter whirls and clatters along
      a tabletop collage of broken glass and coral.

But don't forget too the snow
          and the bridge
      and the man
             who fell, not falls, and that
               never
               changed.

WHY DON'T YOU ANSWER

Let's not call it consequence
    then, when the white
        pages resist an amnesia
        sweeter than tendencies.

    This fragile wealth of injuries,
        who needs it?

Later, and still later.

THEY DON'T BUILD SHIPS FAST ENOUGH
TO CARRY IT AWAY

By luck or so
arrived, "bespoke."

There's little that doesn't count.
A question of address. Tender
without flailing, this won't
                    hurt a bit.

Wrists wrapped in a cello string.

Awake and seeming,
tied to a tree, naked,
screaming the cold
and all it covers. Night was
          never so familiar
          or necessary.

Sorry doesn't cut it when a board
          with 5 rusty nails is
a prophecy or sorts:
                    what'll do for now.

One hallelujah is the common

                    place of time, a second
                    and the edges of your face narrow
                              into

                    a beak, teeth shattered and

honest. Wake to speech
and make the saying slow,
                 until
the bandages come off.

If I could interrogate you, it'd be a deliberate

                 reply: *mea*
culpa's wedged as they are

                 into the hole in the floorboards.

The soles of the leather shoes are cracked.

Indirection is a neon sign, a martini glass.
Lined up along the edges, orderly,
                 this lack, the space between my fingers,

                 becomes the shape of attention.

If seeing you once again means *be still*,

to understand is hard, isn't it? The debt of such dumb,
                                 beautiful measures.

I will say *error* and you will disappear.
I will stutter and you will plummet into the sea.
I will demand and the needle of a phonograph
                                 will go dull and amnesiac.

And by you I mean me.

                 The upstairs window is desperate with loathing.

The plot of failure, parabolic,

castigates and forgives
while a corpse borne out from the dining room
         resists the allegory that wishes it someplace else
something easier

to tick off in columns of the not
              yet daily.

If I called for something more, we
              notice her forearm is soft yet
pathetic in its hinge and succor, is it
       pornographic?
     Write the body towards a chalk outline.
        Appetite/evidence.

           Urine stains petition the daylight,
the dead is dead is here and the dance
     is hitch and step, box two
          and three for the carnival
of what do you figure,
        finger,
          flatter.

Q: What tolerates possession?
A: Variance.

       And in the dark forest of the middle years
   the phrases loosen
and tumble.

It's a good life if you don't weaken. But to be

sent
for is only a first
beginning, the rest staggered,
        who could we
substitute more
better, more blame, not lost
        but misnamed.

This current alternates
this current is direct
this current says I love you
and this current breaks the storefront window.

Bright tongue of silence in a room with the shades drawn.
        We cannot rid ourselves of form: claimed things crowd
the edges. A window is a window and is not enough.

In the event of an emergency
        the book in front of you
can act as a consolation device. Is that funny?

How you like me now? dwindles as it will, one hopes.
A voice, regardless, is
                a continuance
                of a kind.
Irresponsible, the newspaper rasps
across the sidewalk. *What do you know, Joe?*

The moment, as one finds it, is a slaughterhouse.

How much bracket to hold?

Pushed back, denial
      a way of singing out a zero sum.

I want to understand the impossibility of reaching.

Given to being here,
the shoulders
      stiffen in all this rain.

This city's pleasure
      rests against the skin.

Phenoemena almost intends her eye.

            How can you touch
         that which is not
            there all along?

Say it forward, say it backward, say
      it five times fast.

What rough tune calls it forth
      so vacancy pirouettes like a graceless circus bear. You'd
talk

until morning, in order to
      stop talking, to let the voice grow hoarse
               and incidental,
                 and then
      what could follow?
The will to be heard,

the hum and sigh draws us near.

The front room fills with soot and the tiny light of
fugitive things grows late.

The edge of your eyelid is the very integer
of what you hope for. The rest is already packed.

Though we know
a great mineral intent and
            the guilt of staying put,
the building is still glass.

yes is an open page
to survive caring.

Make my way home,
through all this mess.

To say the least / Less / An unspeakable sudden.

Richard Deming is a poet and a theorist who works on the philosophy of literature. His book, *Listening on All Sides: Towards an Emersonian Ethics of Reading,* was published by Stanford University Press in 2007. His poems have appeared in such journals as *Sulfur, Field, Kiosk, Mandorla,* and *Shearsman.* With Nancy Kuhl, he edits Phylum Press (www.phylumpress.com). He is currently a lecturer at Yale University.

Printed in the United States
136452LV00002BA/2/A

9 781905 700660